Walking the Via Dolorosa

A Journey Through the 14 Stations of the Cross

Maundy Thursday Evening

A Journey Through The Stations Of The Cross

Rev. Jimmy Davis

Walking the Via Dolorosa

A Journey Through the 14 Stations of the Cross

CONTENTS

Walking the Via Dolorosa

A Journey Through the 14 Stations of the Cross

About the Author

Reverend Jimmy Davis, 62, has dedicated his life to God with steadfast faith and commitment. His spiritual journey began to evolve in the mid-1990s when he started ministering to the youth in his church. This role not only nurtured his leadership skills but also deepened his passion for serving others, setting the foundation for his future in ministry. As his dedication grew, Davis took on greater responsibilities, eventually becoming an assistant to the pastor—a role that allowed his gifts in ministry to flourish.

By the early 2000s, Davis felt a powerful and undeniable call to pastoral leadership. He answered this call by enrolling in seminary and pursuing biblical studies at Nazarene Bible College, dedicating himself to gaining the knowledge and wisdom needed to guide others in their faith. After completing his studies in 2011, Davis was ordained in the Evangelical Methodist Church in 2012. His pastoral career has since been marked by faithful service as a senior pastor in three different congregations, where he has guided his flocks with compassion and dedication.

In addition to his pastoral responsibilities, Reverend Davis served in public safety, demonstrating his commitment to protecting and serving his community. His dual roles as both a pastor and a public servant have exemplified his heart for service, reflecting his deep love for others. Now retired from public safety, Davis continues to answer God's call, recently being appointed to serve a new congregation this year.

Reverend Davis's personal life is a testament to God's blessings. He has been married to his wife, Kelly, since 1989, and together they share a partnership rooted in love and faith. They have raised two adult children, both of whom are now married, continuing the family legacy of faithfulness.

Reverend Davis's life is a powerful testimony to God's grace, faithfulness, and the transformative power of a life surrendered to His will. Whether through his preaching, his leadership, or his example as a devoted husband and father, Reverend Jimmy Davis continues to make a meaningful impact on the Kingdom of God, inspiring all who encounter his ministry.

Introduction

The **Via Dolorosa**, also known as the "Way of Sorrow" or "Way of Suffering," is a route in the Old City of Jerusalem that is believed to be the path Jesus walked on the way to His crucifixion. This sacred route commemorates the final journey of Jesus from the place of His trial and condemnation by Pontius Pilate to Golgotha, the site of His crucifixion, also known as Calvary.

Key Aspects of the Via Dolorosa:

1. **Historical Significance:**

   o   The Via Dolorosa is traditionally considered the actual path Jesus took on Good Friday. It has been a focus of Christian pilgrimage for centuries, attracting millions of believers who wish to walk in the footsteps of Christ.

2. **Route and Stations:**

   o   The Via Dolorosa starts near the site of the Antonia Fortress, where Jesus was condemned, and ends at the Church of the Holy Sepulchre, which houses the traditional sites of the crucifixion, burial, and resurrection of Jesus.

   o   Along the Via Dolorosa are the **14 Stations of the Cross**, each marking a significant event during Jesus' journey. Some of these stations are based on biblical accounts, while others are rooted in Christian tradition.

3. **Modern Experience:**

   o   Today, the Via Dolorosa winds through narrow streets, bustling markets, and ancient sites in Jerusalem. Pilgrims often carry crosses and stop at each station for prayer and reflection, re-enacting Jesus' final steps.

4. **Significance for Believers:**

   o   The Via Dolorosa serves as a profound spiritual journey for Christians. Walking this path allows believers to physically and emotionally connect with Jesus' suffering and sacrifice, deepening their appreciation of His love and the cost of redemption.

5. **Cultural and Religious Context:**

   o   The route reflects not only Christian history but also the complex religious and cultural landscape of Jerusalem, intersecting with Jewish, Muslim, and Christian traditions.

Study Guide on the Stations of the Via Dolorosa

Preparation: The symbolism of the Candle

As you begin this study, place a lighted candle in the centerpiece of each table. The candle represents the light of Christ and symbolizes His journey through each of the 14 Stations of the Cross. As we reflect on each station, participants will extinguish the candle at their table after the station is completed, representing the growing darkness that Jesus faced on His way to the cross.

Station I: Jesus is Condemned by Pilate

Scripture:

- *"Pilate saith unto them, What shall I do then with Jesus which is called Christ? They all say unto him, Let him be crucified."* — Matthew 27:22 (KJV)

Significance:

Jesus is condemned to death by Pontius Pilate, who yields to the pressure of the crowd despite knowing Jesus' innocence. This station illustrates the world's rejection of Christ, injustice, and the human tendency to avoid responsibility.

Reflection Questions:

1. Why did Pilate condemn Jesus despite finding no fault in Him?

   Answer: Pilate feared the backlash from the crowd and the potential political repercussions, showing how fear and pressure can lead to unjust decisions.

2. What can we learn from Pilate's actions?

   Answer: It teaches us the importance of standing up for truth and justice, even when it is difficult or unpopular.

Action: Extinguish the candle at your table.

Station II: Jesus Takes Up His Cross

Scripture:

- *"And he bearing his cross went forth into a place called the place of a skull, which is called in the Hebrew Golgotha."* — John 19:17 (KJV)

Significance:

Jesus willingly accepts the cross, embracing the burden of humanity's sins. This act demonstrates His obedience to the Father and His love for humanity.

Reflection Questions:

1. How does Jesus' acceptance of the cross inspire you in your own life?

   Answer: It reminds us to bear our burdens with faith and perseverance, trusting in God's plan.

2. What does it mean to "take up your cross" in your daily life?

    Answer: It means living a life of sacrifice, humility, and commitment to following God's will, even in the face of hardship.

Action: Extinguish the candle at your table.

Station III: Jesus Falls the First Time

Scripture:

- *"Surely he hath borne our griefs, and carried our sorrows: yet we did esteem him stricken, smitten of God, and afflicted."* — Isaiah 53:4 (KJV)

Significance:

Jesus' first fall under the weight of the cross reflects His human frailty and the overwhelming burden He carries. It shows His willingness to endure suffering for our sake.

Reflection Questions:

1. What does Jesus' fall teach us about human weakness?

    Answer: It shows that even the strongest can stumble, but what matters is getting back up and continuing to fulfill God's purpose.

2. How can we find strength when we fall in our own lives?

    Answer: We can rely on God's strength, knowing that He understands our struggles and is with us in our trials.

Action: Extinguish the candle at your table.

Station IV: Jesus Meets His Mother, Mary

Scripture:

- *"Yea, a sword shall pierce through thy own soul also, that the thoughts of many hearts may be revealed."* — Luke 2:35 (KJV)

Significance:

The sorrowful meeting between Jesus and Mary highlights the deep emotional pain of a mother watching her son suffer. It reflects the shared suffering and love between Jesus and His mother.

Reflection Questions:

1. How does Mary's presence during Jesus' journey inspire us?

   Answer: Mary's steadfast presence teaches us the power of silent support and the importance of standing by loved ones in their darkest moments.

2. How can we offer comfort to others in their times of suffering?

   Answer: We can be present, offer support, and pray for those who are hurting, showing love and compassion as Mary did.

Action: Extinguish the candle at your table.

Station V: Simon of Cyrene Helps Jesus Carry the Cross

Scripture:

- *"And as they led him away, they laid hold upon one Simon, a Cyrenian, coming out of the country, and on him they laid the cross, that he might bear it after Jesus."* — Luke 23:26 (KJV)

Significance:

Simon of Cyrene is compelled to help Jesus carry the cross. This act shows that we are called to help one another bear life's burdens.

Reflection Questions:

1. What does Simon's help symbolize for us?

    Answer: It represents the call to support each other in times of need, sharing in one another's struggles.

2. How can you be a "Simon" to someone in your life today?

    Answer: By offering help, listening, or simply being present, we can lighten the load of others.

Action: Extinguish the candle at your table.

Station VI: Veronica Wipes the Face of Jesus

Scripture:

*   *"Inasmuch as ye have done it unto one of the least of these my brethren, ye have done it unto me."* — Matthew 25:40 (KJV)

Significance:

According to tradition, Veronica shows compassion by wiping Jesus' face. This small act of kindness reflects the importance of showing love and mercy, even in dire circumstances.

Reflection Questions:

1. How can small acts of kindness make a difference?

Answer: Small acts of kindness can provide comfort and demonstrate love, reminding us that even small gestures matter.

2. How can you show compassion in your daily interactions?

   Answer: By being mindful of others' needs and offering help whenever possible, we can reflect Christ's love.

Action: Extinguish the candle at your table.

Station VII: Jesus Falls the Second Time

Scripture:

- *"For we have not an high priest which cannot be touched with the feeling of our infirmities; but was in all points tempted like as we are, yet without sin."* — Hebrews 4:15 (KJV)

Significance:

Jesus' second fall shows His increasing physical weakness and the toll of carrying the cross. It reflects the perseverance required to continue, even when overwhelmed.

Reflection Questions:

1. What can we learn from Jesus' perseverance?

   Answer: Jesus' determination encourages us to keep going despite repeated failures and challenges, trusting in God's strength.

2. How do you handle moments of weakness and exhaustion?

Answer: By turning to God for strength, seeking support from others, and remembering that persistence is key.

Action: Extinguish the candle at your table.

Station VIII: Jesus Meets the Women of Jerusalem

Scripture:

- *"But Jesus turning unto them said, Daughters of Jerusalem, weep not for me, but weep for yourselves, and for your children."* — Luke 23:28 (KJV)

Significance:

Jesus meets a group of women mourning for Him and redirects their sorrow towards their own need for repentance and awareness of their spiritual state.

Reflection Questions:

1. Why does Jesus redirect the women's grief?

   Answer: Jesus encourages them to reflect on their own lives and the future, emphasizing the importance of repentance and readiness.

2. How can we apply Jesus' warning to our own lives?

   Answer: By examining our hearts, repenting of our sins, and living in a way that honors God's call.

Action: Extinguish the candle at your table.

Station IX: Jesus Falls the Third Time

Scripture:

- *"I am troubled; I am bowed down greatly; I go mourning all the day long."* — Psalm 38:6 (KJV)

Significance:

The third fall represents the culmination of Jesus' physical and emotional suffering. It highlights the heavy burden of sin and the perseverance of Jesus to fulfill His mission despite the overwhelming weight.

Reflection Questions:

1. What does this third fall symbolize in our spiritual journey?

   Answer: It symbolizes that even when we are at our lowest, God's grace enables us to rise again.

2. How can you find strength when you feel completely overwhelmed?

   Answer: By relying on God's promises, seeking His presence, and not giving up despite the difficulties.

Action: Extinguish the candle at your table.

Station X: Jesus is Stripped of His Garments

Scripture:

- *"They parted my garments among them, and upon my vesture did they cast lots."* — John 19:23-24 (KJV)

Significance:

Jesus is stripped of His garments, symbolizing His complete

vulnerability and humility. This act highlights the degradation He endured and His total sacrifice.

Reflection Questions:

1. How does Jesus' stripping reflect His sacrifice?

   Answer: It shows His willingness to endure shame and loss for our redemption, demonstrating His complete surrender for humanity's sake.

2. How can we practice humility in our own lives?

   Answer: By letting go of pride, serving others selflessly, and recognizing that our true worth comes from God.

Action: Extinguish the candle at your table.

Station XI: Jesus is Nailed to the Cross

Scripture:

- *"And when they were come to the place, which is called Calvary, there they crucified him, and the malefactors, one on the right hand, and the other on the left."* — Luke 23:33 (KJV)

Significance:

Jesus is nailed to the cross, enduring unimaginable pain and fulfilling the prophecy of His suffering for the world's sins. This station reflects the depth of His love and the ultimate sacrifice.

Reflection Questions:

1. How does Jesus' crucifixion impact your understanding of His love?

    Answer: It demonstrates the boundless nature of His love, willingness to endure the greatest pain for our salvation.

2. What does it mean to take up your own cross daily?

    Answer: It means to live with a spirit of sacrifice, enduring hardships with faith, and following Christ's example in all areas of life.

Action: Extinguish the candle at your table.

Station XII: Jesus Dies on the Cross

Scripture:

- *"When Jesus therefore had received the vinegar, he said, It is finished: and he bowed his head, and gave up the ghost."* — John 19:30 (KJV)

Significance:

Jesus' death on the cross marks the completion of His earthly mission. His final words, "It is finished," signify the fulfillment of God's plan of salvation and the atonement for humanity's sins.

Reflection Questions:

1. What does "It is finished" mean for our faith?

    Answer: It means that the work of salvation is complete; Jesus paid the price in full, securing redemption for all who believe.

2. How does Jesus' sacrifice inspire you to live differently?

Answer: It calls us to live with gratitude, commitment, and a desire to share His love with others.

Action: Extinguish the candle at your table.

Station XIII: Jesus is Taken Down from the Cross

Scripture:

- *"And he took it down, and wrapped it in linen, and laid it in a sepulchre that was hewn in stone, wherein never man before was laid."* — Luke 23:53 (KJV)

Significance:

Jesus' body is taken down from the cross and placed in the arms of His mother, Mary. This moment reflects the sorrow of His followers and the reality of His death.

Reflection Questions:

1. How does this scene of sorrow speak to you?

   Answer: It shows the depth of loss felt by those who loved Jesus and the human experience of grief.

2. What does this teach us about honoring Christ's sacrifice?

   Answer: It calls us to remember the price He paid and to live in a way that honors His gift of salvation.

Action: Extinguish the candle at your table.

Station XIV: Jesus is Laid in the Tomb

Scripture:

- *"And when Joseph had taken the body, he wrapped it in a clean linen cloth, And laid it in his own new tomb, which he had hewn out in the rock: and he rolled a great stone to the door of the sepulchre, and departed."* — Matthew 27:59-60 (KJV)

Significance:

Jesus is laid in the tomb, marking the end of His earthly suffering. It is a moment of stillness and waiting, symbolizing the hope of resurrection that will soon follow.

Reflection Questions:

1. How does the burial of Jesus inspire hope despite its apparent finality?

   Answer: It reminds us that even in death, there is the promise of resurrection and new life through Christ.

2. What does this station teach us about waiting on God's timing?

   Answer: It encourages us to trust in God's plans, knowing that what seems like the end can be the beginning of something greater.

Action: Extinguish the candle at your table.

Conclusion:

This study guide on the Stations of the Via Dolorosa invites participants to journey alongside Jesus, reflecting deeply on His sacrifice and the profound love He demonstrated. The extinguishing of the candles symbolizes the increasing darkness Jesus endured for our sake, reminding us of the price He paid and the hope that is found in His resurrection. May this study inspire you to live in the light of Christ's love and grace.

Evening Dinner Menu for Maundy Thursday

This menu is inspired by the Last Supper, which was a Passover meal that Jesus shared with His disciples on Maundy Thursday. The meal reflects traditional elements that would have been part of a Jewish Passover Seder during the time of Jesus. The evening will conclude with a foot-washing ceremony and Communion of Remembrance to honor the events of that sacred night.

A Traditional Jewish Passover Meal Menu

1. **Appetizers (Karpas):**

   - **Bitter Herbs (Maror):** Fresh horseradish or romaine lettuce to symbolize the bitterness of slavery in Egypt.

   - **Charoset:** A sweet mixture of apples, nuts, cinnamon, and wine, symbolizing the mortar used by the Israelite slaves.

   - **Matzo (Unleavened Bread):** A staple of the Passover meal, representing the haste in which the Israelites left Egypt, without time for their bread to rise.

   - **Karpas (Parsley or Celery):** Dipped in saltwater, symbolizing tears shed in slavery.

2. **Main Course:**

   - **Roasted Lamb:** The central element of the Passover meal, recalling the lamb whose blood was used during the

Exodus to protect the Israelites. For observance, consider serving a slow-roasted lamb seasoned with herbs and spices.

- **Herbed Chicken or Fish (Optional):** For those who may not eat lamb, a simple roast chicken or fish seasoned with herbs, olive oil, and garlic can be offered as an alternative.

3. **Side Dishes:**

- **Roasted Vegetables:** A mix of root vegetables such as carrots, potatoes, and onions, seasoned with olive oil, rosemary, and thyme.

- **Green Salad with Olive Oil and Vinegar Dressing:** Fresh greens, tomatoes, cucumbers, and olives, dressed simply to complement the meal.

- **Rice Pilaf or Quinoa:** Lightly seasoned with herbs and nuts, adding texture and flavor.

4. **Dessert:**

- **Fruit Compote:** A mix of dried fruits such as dates, figs, and raisins, simmered in wine or juice, spiced with cinnamon and cloves, reflecting the flavors of ancient times.

- **Honey Cake or Almond Cookies:** Light, sweet treats made with honey or nuts, traditionally enjoyed during Jewish celebrations.

5. **Wine (Four Cups of Wine):**

- o Red wine or grape juice to symbolize the four promises of redemption made by God to the Israelites in Exodus 6:6-7.

Significance of the Foot Washing Ceremony

Significance:

- After the meal, follow Jesus' example by holding a foot washing ceremony, demonstrating humility and service to one another (John 13:1-17). This symbolic act reminds us of Jesus' command to love and serve one another.

Procedure:

- Provide a basin of warm water, towels, and chairs. Participants can take turns washing each other's feet or have designated individuals perform the washing.

Only An Ordained Minister can Perform this Sacrament.

Communion of Remembrance

Elements:

- **Unleavened Bread:** Symbolizes Jesus' body broken for us.

- **Red Wine or Grape Juice:** Represents Jesus' blood shed for the forgiveness of sins.

Scripture Reading:

- Read from 1 Corinthians 11:23-26 (KJV): *"For I have received of the Lord that which also I delivered unto you, That the Lord Jesus the same night in which he was betrayed took bread: And when he had given thanks, he brake it, and said, Take, eat: this is my body, which is broken for you: this do in remembrance of me. After the same manner also he took the cup, when he had supped, saying, This cup is the new testament in my blood: this do ye, as oft as ye drink it, in remembrance of me."*

Reflection:

- Reflect on Jesus' sacrifice and His command to love one another. Encourage participants to partake of the bread and wine with reverence, remembering the ultimate price Jesus paid.

This Maundy Thursday evening dinner and ceremony provide a meaningful way to honor the Last Supper, drawing participants into a deeper understanding of Jesus' final hours with His disciples and His powerful acts of love, service, and sacrifice.

Creating the Atmosphere: Music and Ambiance

To create a meaningful and reverent atmosphere for the Maundy Thursday dinner, the music and background should evoke a sense of reflection, reverence, and connection to the sacred events being commemorated. Here are some suggestions for music and ambiance to enhance the evening:

Music Selection for Reflection and Reverence

1. **Music Selection:**

    o **Instrumental Hymns:** Soft, instrumental versions of traditional hymns such as "When I Survey the Wondrous Cross," "Were You There," and "O Sacred Head, Now Wounded." These hymns reflect the themes of sacrifice and redemption.

    o **Classical Sacred Music:** Selections from composers like Johann Sebastian Bach, particularly his "St. Matthew Passion," or Antonio Vivaldi's "Stabat Mater," can create a solemn and meditative environment.

    o **Jewish Traditional Music:** Soft instrumental pieces with traditional Jewish melodies, such as "Eliyahu Hanavi" or "Shalom Aleichem," evoke the cultural context of the Passover meal and connect the evening to its Jewish roots.

- **Gregorian Chants or Taizé Music:** These pieces are deeply contemplative and create a worshipful atmosphere. Songs like "Ubi Caritas" or "Jesus, Remember Me" can be particularly moving and appropriate for the occasion.

2. **Sound Level and Volume:**

- Keep the music at a low, background level to ensure it enhances but does not overpower the conversation or the significance of the evening. The music should serve as a gentle backdrop, inviting reflection without distraction.

3. **Ambient Sounds:**

- **Candlelight and Soft Lighting:** Create a warm and intimate setting with candlelight, reminiscent of an ancient meal setting. Soft, warm lighting adds to the feeling of reverence and reflection.

- **Subtle Nature Sounds:** Low-volume sounds of wind, gentle water, or rustling leaves can add an organic, calming layer to the ambiance, bringing a sense of peace to the room.

4. **Decor and Table Setting:**

- **Simple Table Setting:** Use a white or cream tablecloth, symbolizing purity and humility. Include simple, natural elements like fresh herbs, sprigs of rosemary or thyme, and a few decorative, unscented candles.

- **Rustic Elements:** Incorporate earthenware or wooden serving dishes to reflect the humble nature of the meal Jesus shared with His disciples.

5. **Timing and Transitions:**

   o Begin the evening with soft instrumental music as guests arrive and are seated. As the meal progresses, keep the music playing softly in the background.

   o During the foot washing and Communion, consider playing quieter, more reflective pieces, allowing the focus to shift to these significant acts of remembrance.

Atmosphere and Flow

- The overall atmosphere should encourage quiet conversation, prayerful reflection, and a sense of sacred communion among participants. The setting and music should make everyone feel connected to the historical and spiritual significance of Maundy Thursday, fostering a deep sense of community and reverence for Christ's love and sacrifice.

By carefully selecting the music and setting the right atmosphere, this Maundy Thursday dinner will provide a moving, memorable experience that honors the profound events of the Last Supper and Jesus' final acts of service and sacrifice.

End of Service Reflection

At the conclusion of the Maundy Thursday evening, after the 14 Stations of the Cross have been reflected upon and the foot washing and Communion have taken place, the goal is to create a solemn, reflective atmosphere as the group is dismissed. This final moment should underscore the gravity and significance of Jesus' journey, allowing participants to leave in a contemplative and respectful manner.

1. **Silent Reflection or Soft Chime:**

   - **Moment of Silence:** Conclude with a brief moment of silence, allowing the group to reflect on the evening's experience and internalize the lessons of the 14 Stations. Silence can be powerful, providing a space for personal prayer and meditation.

   - **Soft Chime or Bell:** Gently ring a small chime or bell once or twice at the end of the silence to signal the conclusion. The chime symbolizes the finality of Jesus' journey and sets a respectful tone as the group prepares to depart.

2. **Low, Ambient Music:**

   - **Quiet, Ambient Soundscape:** Play a very soft, ambient soundscape with gentle nature sounds like light wind, rustling leaves, or distant water, evoking a sense of calm and introspection. This can help ease the transition from the reflective time to the end of the evening.

- **Instrumental Lament or Requiem:** A piece of soft, slow instrumental music, such as an instrumental version of "O Sacred Head, Now Wounded" or "Were You There," can provide a gentle, mournful atmosphere that reflects the somberness of the evening.

3. **Dimming of Lights:**

- Gradually dim the lights as the event comes to a close, symbolizing the darkness that fell as Jesus was laid in the tomb. This visual effect can deepen the emotional impact of the evening and remind participants of the somber nature of the events commemorated.

4. **Candle Extinguishing:**

- **Extinguish Candles Slowly:** If candles have been used throughout the evening, extinguish them slowly and one by one. This action symbolizes the closing of the night and the end of Jesus' earthly journey, creating a powerful and poignant moment.

- **Leave One Candle Lit:** Consider leaving one candle lit to symbolize the hope of the resurrection to come, subtly reminding everyone that darkness does not have the final word.

5. **Dismissal with Quiet Blessing:**

- Conclude with a simple, quiet blessing or benediction. Something like, "May the peace of Christ, who bore our sorrows, go with you tonight," spoken softly, will help guide the group into a contemplative departure.

6. **Encourage Quiet Departure:**

- o Invite participants to leave in silence or soft whispers, maintaining the atmosphere of reflection as they exit. Remind them that this evening is a time for personal contemplation and prayerful remembrance of Christ's sacrifice.

Atmospheric Effects as Participants Leave:

- As participants exit, maintain the subdued lighting and continue the ambient music until everyone has left. This helps sustain the atmosphere of reverence and respect, ensuring that the mood remains reflective and solemn even as the group disperses.

These carefully chosen sound effects and visual cues will help close the evening in a way that honors the gravity of the events commemorated, allowing each person to carry the lessons of the evening into their hearts as they leave.

Setup Guide for a Maundy Thursday Service in the Fellowship Hall

This setup creates a meaningful and reflective atmosphere for a Maundy Thursday service, emphasizing the journey of Jesus through the Stations of the Cross. Each table represents a station, with a central table symbolizing the final moments of Jesus' journey.

Room Layout and Table Arrangement

1. **Table Arrangement:**

   - **13 Round Tables**: Arrange the 13 round tables in a circular or semi-circular formation around the room. Each table represents one of the first 13 Stations of the Cross.

   - **1 Central Table**: Place a single table in the center of the room, slightly elevated or distinguished to stand out, representing the 14th Station, where Jesus is laid in the tomb.

2. **Table Setup:**

   - **Tables 1-13**:

     - Place a white tablecloth on each table to symbolize purity and solemnity.

- In the center of each table, place a single lit candle to represent the light of Christ during His journey through the Stations of the Cross.

- Consider placing a small, simple card or sign on each table indicating which station it represents (e.g., "Station I: Jesus is Condemned by Pilate," "Station II: Jesus Takes Up His Cross," etc.).

- Add a small Bible or scripture card with relevant verses for each station for participants to reflect upon during the service.

3. **Central Table (14th Station):**

   - **Candle Setup**: Place a single, larger candle in the center of this table to symbolize Christ's presence and His ultimate sacrifice. This candle will be extinguished at the end of the service, marking the somber conclusion of Maundy Thursday.

   - **Decoration**: Use minimal decoration, such as a dark tablecloth, to contrast the white ones on the surrounding tables, emphasizing the somber theme of Jesus being laid in the tomb.

Additional Setup Elements

1. **Lighting:**

   - Use dimmed lighting to create a reflective and solemn atmosphere, focusing attention on the candles at each table. Soft, warm lighting can help to enhance the contemplative mood of the evening.

    o If possible, use overhead spotlights or subtle lighting to highlight the central table, drawing the participants' focus to the final station.

2. Seating:

    o Arrange 4-6 chairs around each table, allowing participants to sit together and reflect on each station. Encourage small group discussion or quiet reflection as the service progresses.

3. Sound and Music:

    o Soft, instrumental music or hymns can be played quietly in the background to maintain a reverent atmosphere. Consider pieces like "O Sacred Head, Now Wounded" or "When I Survey the Wondrous Cross."

    o A microphone can be set up near the central table for readings or prayers to be led by the service leader.

4. Service Flow:

    o Begin the service by introducing the significance of the 14 Stations and the symbolism of the candles.

    o As each station is reflected upon, participants will extinguish the candle at their table, marking the progression of Jesus' journey to the cross.

    o After the final reflection on Station XIII (Jesus is taken down from the cross), gather attention to the central table.

- Extinguish the central candle at the end of the service, symbolizing Jesus being laid in the tomb and the conclusion of Maundy Thursday.

Final Touches

- **Quiet Reflection Time:** Allow a few moments of silence after the final candle is extinguished to let participants reflect on the events and the significance of the evening.

- **Dismissal:** Encourage participants to leave quietly, maintaining the atmosphere of reverence and reflection.

This setup provides a deeply symbolic and engaging environment that allows participants to journey with Christ through the Stations of the Cross, fostering a powerful sense of connection to the events of Maundy Thursday.

Reflection on the Maundy Thursday Service: The Way of the Cross

The Maundy Thursday service, centered around the 14 Stations of the Cross, is more than just a historical reenactment; it is a profound journey that invites each of us to walk alongside Jesus in His final moments. This service is designed to help us reflect deeply on Christ's sacrifice, the gravity of His love, and what it means to follow Him in our daily lives.

As each candle is extinguished, symbolizing the increasing darkness that Jesus endured, we are drawn into the heart of His Passion. This moment-by-moment journey not only recounts the physical suffering of Christ but also serves as a powerful reminder of the spiritual and emotional burdens He bore for each of us.

What This Service Should Mean to You as a Participant

1. **A Deep Connection to Christ's Suffering and Sacrifice:**

   - Each station represents a significant moment in Jesus' journey to the cross, reminding us of His unwavering commitment to the Father's will. As we reflect on these moments, we are called to consider our own lives—our struggles, our crosses, and the ways we are invited to walk in Christ's footsteps. The extinguishing of each candle is a solemn reminder that Jesus' light was willingly dimmed for our sake, drawing us closer to understanding the depth of His sacrifice.

2. **An Invitation to Humility and Repentance:**

   - Maundy Thursday is a powerful call to examine our hearts, acknowledging our own sins and shortcomings. Just as Christ humbly accepted the cross, we too are invited to lay down our pride, confess our sins, and turn back to God with a renewed spirit. This service is a reminder that true discipleship often involves suffering, humility, and the willingness to carry our own crosses.

3. **A Shared Journey of Compassion and Community:**

   - The Via Dolorosa is not just Jesus' path; it is ours as well. Along His journey, Jesus encountered those who shared in His suffering—His mother Mary, Simon of Cyrene, and the women of Jerusalem. In these moments, we see the importance of compassion, support, and shared sorrow. As participants, we are reminded that we do not journey alone; we are part of a community that supports one another in times of darkness, just as Jesus was supported on His way to Calvary.

4. **A Reminder of the Profound Love of Christ:**

   o At each station, Jesus demonstrates the boundless nature of His love—a love that endures betrayal, mockery, and unimaginable pain. This service invites us to meditate on that love, allowing it to penetrate our hearts and inspire us to live differently. The extinguishing candles are a symbol of the light that Jesus willingly gave up, reflecting the ultimate act of love: laying down His life for us.

5. **A Moment of Silence, Anticipation, and Hope:**

   o As the final candle is extinguished at the end of the service, we are left in darkness, reflecting on the weight of Jesus' death. Yet, this darkness is not without hope. Maundy Thursday leaves us in a place of quiet anticipation, reminding us that, though the cross represents loss, it also sets the stage for the resurrection. This service challenges us to carry that hope into our own lives, trusting that God's light can never truly be extinguished.

Personal Reflection

- **How did the service impact you?** Allow the emotions stirred by this service—sorrow, gratitude, reflection—to deepen your relationship with Christ. Let this be a moment where you connect personally with His suffering, knowing that His journey was taken out of love for you.

- **How will you carry the lessons of the cross into your daily life?** As you leave, consider how you can live in a way that honors Christ's sacrifice. Let His love guide your actions, your words, and your heart as you seek to serve Him and others.

Conclusion

This Maundy Thursday service is a sacred reminder of the price Jesus paid and the love He displayed. It calls us to remember, reflect, and respond. As we journey through each station, let us be transformed by the light of Christ, even in moments of darkness, holding on to the hope of the resurrection that is to come. May this time draw you closer to the heart of our Savior and inspire you to walk faithfully in His ways.